CARVING SMALL CHARACTERS IN WOOD

REAR

FRONT

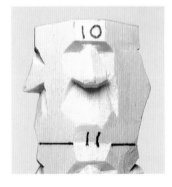

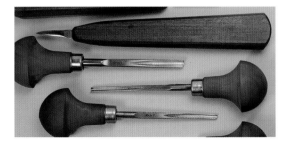

CARVING SMALL CHARACTERS IN WOOD

INSTRUCTIONS & PATTERNS FOR COMPACT PROJECTS WITH PERSONALITY

Jack Price

With Carvings
and Photos by
Jose Gamero

FOX CHAPEL
PUBLISHING
www.FoxChapelPublishing.com

Carving Small Characters in Wood is an updated edition of *Carving Small Characters,* published in 1996 by Weasel Publishing Co. The patterns contained herein are copyrighted by the author. Readers may make copies of these patterns for personal use. The patterns themselves, however, are not to be duplicated for resale or distribution under any circumstances. Any such copying is a violation of copyright law.

ISBN 978-1-4971-0018-3

Studio photography by Mike Mahalo: pages ii (top right character), v–vi, 9, 10, 11 (except for bottom right), 12–16, 22, 33, 43, 50–51, 53, 56, 63, 65, 67, 75, 79, 81, 83, 84, 86–106, and front cover (except for quarter). Character names and step-by-step photography by Jose Gamero. Additional photos by Jose Gamero: pages ii (left three photos and bottom), 11 (bottom right), 17, 25, 59, 73, and back cover (bottom three photos). All carvings by Jose Gamero except those pictured on pages 10, 43, 75, 81, 86, 92–93, and 98–99. Shutterstock: Front cover quarter/Spiroview Inc; page 55 paintbrushes/Zadorozhnyi Viktor.

Library of Congress Cataloging-in-Publication Data

Names: Price, Jack (Jack A.), author.
Title: Carving small characters : creating wooden caricature figurines / Jack Price.
Description: Updated edition. | Mount Joy, PA : Fox Chapel Publishing, 2019. | Revision of: Carving small characters. -- Celburne, Tex. : Weasel Pub., 1996. | Includes bibliographical references. | Summary: "Caricature carver Jack Price shows his process for creative small wooden figurines. Includes step-by-step projects and tips for finishing carvings"-- Provided by publisher.
Identifiers: LCCN 2019024076 | ISBN 9781497100183 (paperback)
Subjects: LCSH: Wood-carving. | Wood-carved figurines.
Classification: LCC TT199.7 .P73 2019 | DDC 736/.4--dc23
LC record available at https://lccn.loc.gov/2019024076

To learn more about the other great books from Fox Chapel Publishing, or to find a retailer near you, call toll-free 800-457-9112 or visit us at *www.FoxChapelPublishing.com*.

We are always looking for talented authors. To submit an idea, please send a brief inquiry to acquisitions@foxchapelpublishing.com.

Printed in China
First printing

To LaMonne, my raison d'etre.

TABLE OF CONTENTS

Carving 202—Post Graduate

PREFACE

The purpose of this book is to teach the reader how to carve small human figures from blocks of wood using a limited assortment of tools. Throughout the book there are pictures and text that show and describe how to make the cuts that produce delightful small characters.

This book is divided into four parts. Part one, Carving 101, includes some rudimentary information about tools, wood, and carving cuts. Experienced carvers will find this portion superfluous and may want to skip ahead.

The second section, Carving 102, describes in detail how to carve the body of a small person, how to carve a face, and how to dress and paint the character.

The third section, Carving 201, portrays ways to carve more sophisticated characters. The information in this section will enable the carver to make the face and head more interesting by adding parts, making facial alterations, and repositioning the head.

The last section, Carving 202, contains the Rogues Gallery and information that will be helpful to those who seek excellence in character carving.

This book describes the way I carve small characters. It is not *THE* way; it is *MY* way. I have tried diligently to take the reader from a pattern on a block of wood to a carved character that makes people smile.

Some of the cuts that I advise will produce parts of a character that are not anatomically correct. Of course, a 2 in. (51 mm) carving of a person with a head that is one-third the length of the total piece is usually not considered to be a "realistic" carving. The only requirement for these little people is that they must be "cute" or "darling" or some such adjective. These are some of the words that people who buy my carvings use to describe them. Of course, I agree with them wholeheartedly.

Good Luck!!!

My Pedagogical Beliefs

In the years that I have taught people to carve small characters, my students have taught me many things. It is the same with this book. I tried my very best to write a book that a neophyte carver, who could read and follow instructions, could carve a satisfactory character just by following the written instructions and studying the pictures.

ACKNOWLEDGMENTS

Special thanks to Bill Gilbert, my good friend of many years, who encouraged, exhorted, goaded, and nagged this ne'er-do-well to complete this book. In desperation he made me an offer I couldn't refuse—free word processing and consultation. I accepted gratefully.

Thanks also to members of the Caricature Carvers of America, a group of carvers so awesomely talented that my association with them has stimulated me to aim a bit higher.

Additional thanks to my many carving friends who encouraged me to complete the book by constantly asking, "When the X@c*% will the new book be available?"

Special thanks to Melvin Mar and Debbie Welch, two graphic design experts, whose know-how, creativity, and artistic ability elevated the appearance of this book from ho-hum to something special.

Jose Gamero, Carver

In 2014, Jose Gamero had developed an interest in wood carving and was looking for the opportunity to start. By coincidence, he discovered Jack Price's legendary book *Carving Small Characters*. Jose absorbed every word Jack put into his book, and since then he has not stopped carving little characters and other figures. Jose's carvings and photographs made this new edition possible.

Dough

CARVING 101
GETTING STARTED

WHY CARVE SMALL CHARACTERS?

1. They are fun to carve.
2. Carving these little characters is energy efficient. The process does not require great strength and large muscles are not overworked.
3. Carving small is environmentally friendly; very little wood is used per character.
4. The cost of wood is minimal. They can even be carved from other people's scrap wood.
5. It is often easier to find 1 in. (25 mm) basswood than it is to find thicker wood.
6. Only a few tools are needed to complete a project.
7. Each character can be completed in a short period of time.
8. If you mess up a carving you can toss the piece away and start another character without feeling a loss of time or money.
9. Carving compact characters can be done almost anywhere. If you carry a piece of wood and a sharp pocketknife with you whenever you are away from home you can make idle time more enjoyable.
10. Small carvings make excellent gifts. They can be produced in a short time and each is highly prized by the recipients.

11. They make good prototypes for larger carvings. If you want to do a large character, do a small one first. Work out some of the problems on a small, inexpensive piece of wood rather than goofing up a large expensive piece.

12. If you sell your carvings you will find that people who would ordinarily not purchase a carving because of the expense, will buy small character carvings because they are affordable.

13. Small character carvings take up very little display space.

14. The variety of characters you can make from the patterns is limited only by your imagination.

15. Carving compact characters helps you make friends. Compact characters are very popular people. They are great conversation starters.

16. People who buy them love them and treasure them. They become collector's items.

17. They make people smile.

18. Carving them relieves stress and makes the carver a better person to be around.

19. Small person character carving slows down the aging process, refreshes the spirit, counters depression, and frees the mind.

20. People who carve small characters stay young in spirit.

Russell

Hermes

BASIC INFORMATION

This portion of the book is written specifically for the beginning carver—the person who wants to carve but is a tad short on "know-how." It is not a treatise on beginning woodcarving but it contains the basic information that I think a novice woodcarver needs to know before attempting a first carving.

Wood

Almost all general-information carving books have a chapter about carving wood. These books identify several woods that are suitable for carving. Talk to experienced carvers and they will give you information about different woods that you may want to try sometime. **For this project I suggest that you obtain a piece of 1 in. (25 mm) basswood and cut it into 2 in. (51 mm) long blocks of wood.** A compact character can be carved from each of these blocks.

One-inch basswood is usually only $^{13}/_{16}$ in. (21 mm) thick. You will find some that is only ¾ in. (19 mm) thick and others that are a full inch. Any size will do but the $^{13}/_{16}$ in. (21 mm) fits the basic man pattern better.

When you price basswood you may think it is expensive. Actually it isn't when you carve small characters. From one board foot of lumber—12 × 12 × 1 in. (30 × 30 cm × 25 mm) you can saw seventy-eight "little people" blocks.

If you have friends who carve medium to large pieces, ask them to save their scrap lumber for you. Most carvers will be delighted to do so because they hate to throw away wood. You will be surprised how many 2 in. (51 mm) blocks of wood you can cut from wood that was worthless to someone else.

One more suggestion. Whenever possible buy kiln-dried wood. It is usually more uniform and cuts better than air-dried wood. Buy northern basswood if you can. When you carve compact characters the quality of wood you select determines the excellence of the finished product to a large degree.

Grain

Wood is made up of layers of microscopic fibers that run the length of the tree. When we speak of grain, we refer to the direction in which the wood fibers are aligned.

It is easy to tell the direction the grain runs when wood is in a rough state. If it "has its hair on" the grain is evident. Basswood that has been planed smooth is more difficult because some basswood is so clear that the grain is hidden.

The easiest way to determine the direction of the grain is by making a cut in the wood. If the knife meets only a little resistance and the cut surface is smooth and shiny, the cut is with the grain. If there is resistance and the surface is rough after the cut is made, the cut is against the grain. **Whenever possible, carve with the grain.** If you have to carve against the grain do so very carefully or you may cut away a large chunk of wood that is essential to the carving.

Cuts that are made across the grain require more force than cuts made with the grain because there is more resistance. However, across-the-grain cuts can be smooth if they are made with sharp tools.

Experienced carvers have learned to test the degree of sharpness of their gouges by making cross-grain cuts. If the cuts are clean and smooth the tool is sharp. If the cuts are ragged and tear the wood, the tool needs to be resharpened. This is an excellent test for V-tools.

Wayne

Sharpening

Another critical factor that determines the success or failure of a woodcarving project is the degree of sharpness of the tools that the carver uses. **Sharp tools that are properly maintained are a pleasure to use** because they produce clean, shiny cuts.

Dull tools are dangerous to use because they require excessive pressure to push the edge through the wood. Dull, and even semi-sharp tools produce cuts that look fuzzy and indistinct. Many would-be carvers lose interest in this wonderful hobby because they do not have sharp carving tools. Carving, for them, becomes an unpleasant chore rather than the enjoyable experience it should be.

Most carving tools, including some knives, are not sharp when they are purchased. It is the rare beginner who can get tools sharp enough to cut wood cleanly. Actually, few experienced carvers are completely satisfied with the degree of sharpness of their tools. Anytime a new sharpening system comes on the market, carvers line up to buy it, hoping it will get their tools a little bit sharper than the system they presently use.

When I consider the purchase of a new tool, I select one that the seller says is sharp. I cut with it on a practice piece of wood to test its keenness and to determine if it fits my hand comfortably.

After the purchase I maintain the sharpness by buffing it on one of several buffing wheels I own or strop it on a piece of leather mounted on a board.

Eventually the tool will lose its edge. When a knife becomes dull, I use a diamond-impregnated steel hone to resharpen it.

I place the knife blade flat on the hone and move it back and forth several times on that side. I reverse the side and repeat the process on the other side. Eventually, if I repeat this process enough times, the stone will wear away the edge of the blade and a fine burr or wire edge will form.

When the burr can be seen and felt along the entire length of the edge of the blade I use a strop or a hard buffing wheel to remove the burr. When the burr is gone the knife is sharp.

With gouges I use one of several abrasive wheels that I own to produce the burr, then remove the burr with the hard buffing wheel.

There are as many sharpening systems as there are carvers. You will have to find one that suits you.

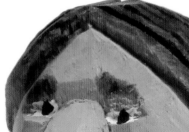

Tools

If you do not have a supply of tools, the suggestions that follow might help you avoid the pitfalls that many inexperienced carvers fall into when purchasing tools.

If you are considering buying tools from an individual or a firm and they will not sharpen them for you before selling them to you, deal with someone else. If that is not feasible, look at the various pre-sharpened tools that are sold at craft stores. They can be honed to a finer edge and are much better for you than tools you have to sharpen, unless you are an expert sharpener.

If you are buying tools for the first time resist the urge to buy everything that looks good to you. Most experienced carvers have a drawer or two of tools they never use. **Buy only what you need.** If you restrict your carving to small characters, the list of tools you will need will be short.

You can carve these little guys with just a knife. However, a few additional tools, such as the ones pictured below, will enable you to create better characters.

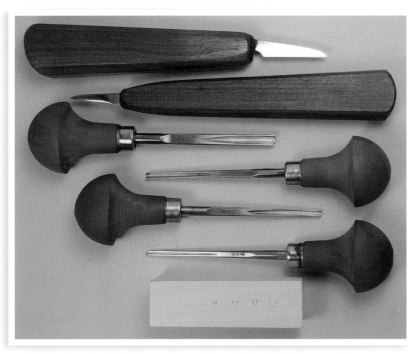

From top: regular carving knife, skinny knife, ¼ in. (6 mm) V-tool, ⅛ in. (3 mm) V-tool, ⅛ in. (3 mm) U-gouge "nostril gouge"

Shown above is a regular carving knife. There are many good commercial knives on the market and many individuals make and sell their own designs. Some of these are superb. If you have the opportunity to attend a woodcarving show, check the dealers to ascertain what is for sale.

Ask individual carvers what tools they recommend. Try tools out before you buy. Be sure they are sharp and comfortable to use.

The second knife above has a long skinny blade. It doesn't need to be this long but it does need to be this skinny. I use this knife to carve the crown of the hat and to make brow cuts. In addition, it is invaluable when I separate the legs of my characters.

The third tool is a ¼ in. (6 mm), or 60 Degree, V-tool. Any V-tool that is similar to this in size will do the job if it is sharp.

You can make hair with your knife or the ¼ in. (6 mm) V-tool but a ⅛ in. (3 mm) V-tool like the one pictured here is better. I find this tool very useful and recommend that you acquire one.

The next tool in the picture is a ⅛ in. (3 mm) U-gouge. It is not an essential tool but I use it to clean out fuzzies from around the bottom of the crown.

I use the last gouge to cut nostrils. You can cut nostrils with a knife but you can also cut off a nose while attempting to do it that way.

There are two other items that I urge you to purchase and use. If you do not have one, purchase a carving glove and use it every time you carve. Using a glove may seem awkward at first but if you use one on a regular basis for a short time you will feel uneasy carving without it on your hand. If you can't find a carving glove, go to a sporting goods store and purchase a fish fillet glove. It's just as good and may be less expensive.

The second purchase that I recommend is a box of rubber fingertips. These are items that office and bank personnel use when they handle paper and/or paper money. The tips can be purchased in an office supply store and come in several sizes. If you wear one on your thumb you will not nick yourself when you make slicing cuts toward your thumb.

I cut the top portion from a tip so it will fit over my right index finger. I wear it just below the second knuckle of my finger at a point where I put a lot of pressure when I carve with a knife. It eases the pressure considerably.

One more bit of advice I'd like to pass on to every carver who reads this book. If you have not had a tetanus shot in the past six years—get one now. If you carve you will cut yourself occasionally and carving tools are not sterile instruments. Even the dullest tools will cut flesh and the chance of a cut getting infected is always present. Don't risk it—get the shot.

Carving Cuts

Many authors of carving books assume that their readers understand what they mean when they suggest a certain cut. My teaching experience tells me that assumption is false, so I have attempted to define five cuts I use.

In-and-Up Cut

This cut is made by pushing a portion of the knife blade, usually the outer ¼ in. (6 mm) of it, straight into the wood then turning the blade and pulling it upward at a 90 degree angle or as close to 90 degrees as you can get. This is the cut I recommend you use when carving the crown of a hat. An example of this cut is shown in **Fig. 3. Figs. 4** and **5** are examples of what can be achieved using this cut and a skinny-bladed knife.

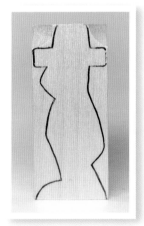

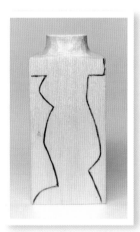

Figure 3   Figure 4   Figure 5

Slicing Cut

This cut has many names. It's called the whittling cut, the straight cut, the rough cut, and the log peeler. I've even heard it called the thumb slicer.

The cut is designed to take off a piece of wood from one point to another and is done with a single stroke. The knife blade is pulled or pushed through the wood in a slicing motion at whatever depth the carver desires.

Whittlers use this cut when they are just making shavings or peeling bark. Shaving makers usually cut away from themselves—a push cut.

When the cutting action is directed toward the carver it's a pull cut. I prefer the pull cut because I feel more in control of the knife when I execute the cut in this manner.

When you make slicing cuts toward your carving hand you should wear some sort of thumb guard on that hand and keep some wood between your thumb and the knife blade.

If you prefer to cut away from your body I recommend that you use the thumb of your non-carving hand to push the blade through the wood. It will give you better control.

Jim Cocke, in his book *Caricature Faces by the Hundreds*, recommends that beginning carvers practice making this cut by rounding off the end of a practice stick. That's very good advice from a great teacher.

A good example of a slicing cut is shown in **Figs. 12** and **13.** Before these cuts were made another cut had to be made. A stop cut, like the one described below, was made just below the hat brim.

Stop Cut

To execute this cut the knife blade is pushed into the wood to a depth that the carver thinks is sufficient to "stop" a second cut made into the first one from another direction. If done correctly, the second cut will cause a chip of wood to pop out. If done incorrectly the second cut will go beyond the stop cut and take out some wood that is, perhaps, vital to your carving. Some of my guys that started out with hats wound up with caps or with hair only because of inadequate stop cuts.

Figure 12

Figure 13

V-Cut or Notch Cut

This cut is a version of the stop cut. The blade is pushed into the wood at a predetermined angle and depth. Into this cut a second cut is made from the opposite direction that is identical in angle and depth to the first one.

Like the stop cut, if the two cuts are properly made, a wedge of wood will pop out and the surface where the wood was removed will be clean. If the two cuts do not meet precisely, there will be fuzzies.

Practice this cut on the edge of a practice stick until the chips pop out clean consistently.

Examples of V-cuts can be found in **Fig. 60.** The brow cuts and the eye cuts on the practice face stick are small V-cuts. Another example is shown in step 10 of the face stick (**Fig. 63**) when the eyes are recut. These cuts are a little deeper and must be done cleanly or that portion of the face will be indistinct.

Straight-in Cut

This cut is made with the tip of the blade. The tip is pushed straight into the wood at a 90 degree angle. A good example of this cut is shown in **Fig. 60.** The three straight-in cuts on each side of the nose form the triangular cut described in the illustration.

Now if you have absorbed all the general information knowledge that you need and if you have practiced the five cuts until they are perfected, it's time to carve the Basic Man described in the next section.

Ezequiel

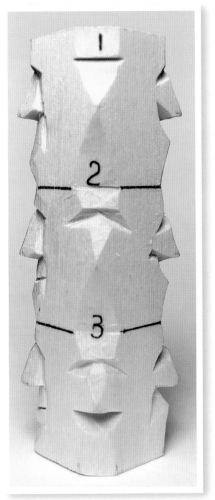

Figure 60

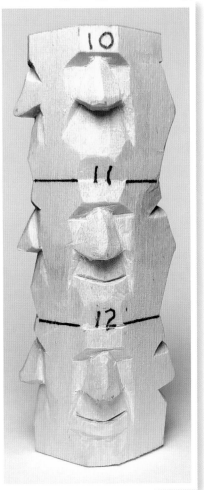

Figure 63

CARVING 102
CARVING THE BASIC MAN

CARVING THE BODY

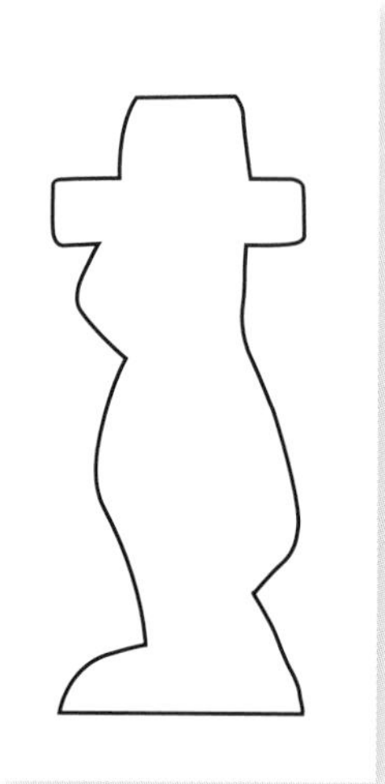

Step 1: The Pattern

The Basic Man is carved from the adjacent pattern. Put a piece of tracing paper over the pattern and trace the outline. Transfer this pattern to a piece of poster board or some like material and cut out the pattern. Trace this pattern on one side of one of your 2 in. (51 mm) blocks of wood. Be sure the pattern runs with the grain of the block. Move the pattern to the opposite side of the block and trace the pattern on that side. The toes and the nose of your pattern should point in the same direction on the two sides of the block of wood.

You are ready now to begin carving your basic man. Follow the directions carefully and observe the pictures and you should be able to carve an acceptable character on the first try.

Step 2: Carving the Hat

When I carve the Basic Man the first cuts are directed toward shaping the crown of the hat. With a narrow, thin-blade knife or the outer ½ in. (13 mm) of your knife blade, make an "in-and-up" cut at each corner of the block of wood. Start on the line that denotes the top of the hat brim. Cut straight into the wood then roll the knife blade toward the top of the hat and continue your cut through the top of the wood. Examples of this cut are shown in **Fig. 3.**

Figure 2

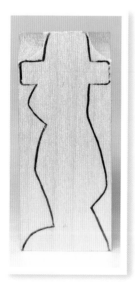

Figure 3

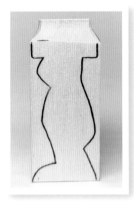

Figure 4

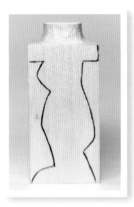

Figure 5

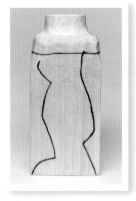

Figure 6

Make this an "in-and-up" cut around the block of wood at the hat brim line. After going around the block once making these cuts, your character should look like **Fig. 4.**

Continue making these cuts around the crown of the hat until your piece looks like **Fig. 5.** To achieve this look you must emphasize the "in" part of the "in and up" stroke. We want the hat crown to be perpendicular to the hat brim with all cuts going up from the hat brim. Never cut down from the top; it doesn't look as good as the "up" cuts if they are done properly with a skinny knife.

Note the rounded top of the crown.

After the crown of your hat looks like the one in **Fig. 5** you make slicing cuts at each corner that angle upward and slightly toward the center. After you make the corner cuts you will have to make cuts on either side of these cuts in order to achieve roundness. These cuts start about ⅜ in. (10 mm) below the brim line. The cuts begin shallow and become deeper at the crown.

When the brim is round, draw a line around the block that is ⅛ in. (3 mm) below the top of the brim. This line denotes where you will make the cuts that will create the bottom of the brim. **Fig. 6** shows the rounded brim with the bottom brim line drawn. You will notice that part of the pattern has been cut away. Don't worry about that: you won't need the part that was cut off.

You can cut the bottom of the hat brim two ways. The easiest way is to cut about ⅛ in. (3 mm) deep into the wood on the line you drew, using a ¼ in. (6 mm) V-tool. The second way is to make a series of V-cuts with your knife blade around the bottom brim line.

These cuts should be ⅛ in. (3 mm) deep and should obliterate the line. Compare your completed cuts to those exhibited in **Fig. 7.**

Step 3: Shaping the Lower Body

Look at **Fig. 8**. Note that cuts have been made at the front of the block that define the feet and the lower abdomen. To achieve this effect, make a stop cut at one of the front corners at the shoe line. Now make a cut that starts from the lower abdomen line and goes to the stop cut. This should take out a nice-sized piece of wood.

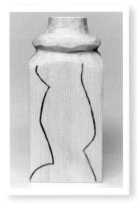

Figure 7

This procedure will require a series of cuts to achieve the pictured look.

Make the same cuts at the other front corner, then make a series of like cuts across the front of the block until your piece looks like the one in **Fig. 8**. Be very careful while making these cuts. You are dealing with cross-grain wood that breaks off easily.

Look at the rear portion of **Fig. 8**. By taking out this wood at the back of the character a buttocks was formed and the legs were defined.

The first cut is made on a corner of the block. It slants downward on the pattern line that denotes the buttocks and stops where the buttocks join the thigh. Make this same cut on the other corner then clean out the wood between these cuts.

Figure 8

These cuts are like the ones at the front of the character. You can be a little bolder with these cuts.

If you made the right cuts in this step, the legs of your character slant from the front to rear, the feet and the buttocks are defined, and you are ready to shape the rest of the body.

Step 4: Shaping the Upper Body

This is a very important step. If it is done correctly the forward portion of the body and the face of your character will be angular rather than square.

Look at **Fig. 9.** There is a perpendicular line, line A, drawn on the block that runs from the bottom of the hat brim to the base of the figure. The line bisects that side of the body. Draw a similar line on your piece.

In **Fig. 10** there are two lines, B and C, that are drawn with about ⅛ in. (3 mm) separating them. Duplicate these lines on the front of your character. The slight gap between lines B and C is intentional. The gap insures that ample wood will be available when the nose is carved.

Fig. 11 shows a fourth line, line D, that is drawn down the center of the left side. Draw this line on your figure. Very carefully remove the wood between lines A and B and the wood between lines C and D. **Figs. 12** and **13** illustrate how the block will look at the conclusion of step 4.

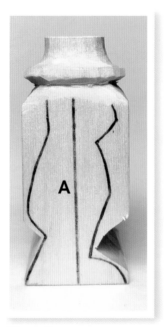

Figure 9

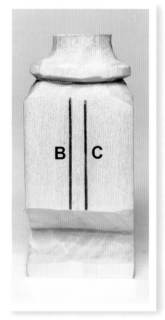

Figure 10

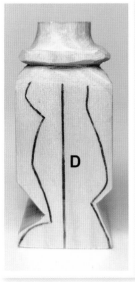

Figure 11

Figure 12

Figure 13

The first cuts you must make are stop cuts under the hat brim on the front portion of the character. Into these cuts make long slicing cuts that start just above the top of the shoes. Do not try to take out this wood with single cuts on each side. Instead, make a series of thin cuts until the waste wood has been removed.

When all the cuts are made, the body, from the shoe tops to the hat brim, should slant backward from line B to line A and from line C to line D.

If you could look at the carving from above and the hat was not in the way, the A B line and the C D line would resemble the dashed lines in **Fig. 14.**

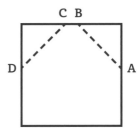

Figure 14

Step 5: Defining the Head

Figs. 15 and **16** show a line that circles the upper portion of the carving. This line denotes where the head will be located.

On the forward surface draw a short horizontal line in the center of the figure that is 1½ in. (38 mm) from the bottom of the brim. Make a similar mark in the back of the object ¼ to ⅜ in. (6 to 10 mm) below the hat brim. Connect these two marks with a continuous line.

If you will study **Figs. 15** and **16** you will observe that several cuts have been made on the piece. **Fig. 15** shows clearly the cut that defines the bridge of the nose. The upper end of the cut is about equal in depth to the crown of the hat. The lower end of the cut is where the end of the nose will be located.

Further scrutiny of the illustrations, especially **Fig. 16,** will lead you to discover that cuts on the sides and at the back of the piece have been made. These cuts slant upward. They were made so it will appear that the person's hair is coming from under the crown of the hat.

Make your character look like the one portrayed in **Figs. 15** and **16.**

Figure 15

Figure 16

Figs. 17 and 18 illustrate the next action you are to take. The first part of the process is to make a rather deep V-cut in the front, with your knife, that will separate the chin from the chest. The cut should be at least ³⁄₁₆ in. (5 mm) deep.

After you make this cut, use your ¼ in. (6 mm) V-gouge to cut a groove around the rest of the body on the "head" line. This groove should be ¹⁄₁₆–³⁄₃₂ in. (1.5–2 mm) deep. Instead of using a V-gouge to make this cut, you can accomplish the same results by making a series of V-cuts on this line with your knife. Look at Figs. 17 and 18 again. When the line that defines the head was cut, a ridge was left below the V-cut. You want to eliminate this ridge. Figs. 19 and 20 show the character after the ridge has been removed. With your knife, make your carving look like the example.

Figure 17

Figure 18

Figure 19

Figure 20

Step 6: More Shoe / Leg Action

Turn your carving so you are looking at the bottom of the block with the front side pointing downward, as in **Fig. 21**. Duplicate the lines that are shown in the illustration on your carving. At the upper end the marks are ⅛ in. (3 mm) from the corners.

The chore now is to remove the wood that is outside the lines you drew. The cuts start at the bottom of the buttocks cut. After you make the cuts, compare your piece with **Fig. 22.**

Now slightly round the back part of your carving on the sides from the buttocks to the shoulders. Also, be sure there is no hump on the back of your character at the shoulder level. You do not want him to look like Quasimodo, the misshapen bell ringer in Victor Hugo's *The Hunchback of Notre Dame.*

Check your carving with the one in **Fig. 23.**

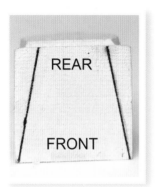

Figure 21

Figure 22

Figure 23

Thomas
and Marvin

Step 7: Carving the Arms

Draw the arms on your character as nearly as possible to those in **Fig. 24.** It is very important that your drawings are as similar to the example as possible. Lines A and B should be parallel to one another and line C should be parallel to the back of the body.

Figs. **25** and **26** show the first cuts in carving the arms. Make a deep stop cut on line B (**Fig. 25**) then make a straight cut into the stop cut from below and remove that wood. This cut should be about ⅛ in. (3 mm) deep at the elbow and should just touch the pocket line. **Fig. 26** shows this cut from the rear.

Fig. **27** pictures the cuts that go from the armpit to the elbow. These are thin notch cuts. After you make these cuts, round the buttocks area.

Many carvings are ruined because the arms are goofy looking. Study Figure 24 VERY carefully, reading the instructions BEFORE you draw the arms on the wood. If they do not look like the ones in Figures 24 and 25, REDRAW them until they look right.

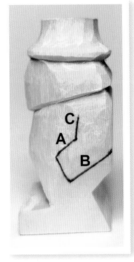

Figure 24

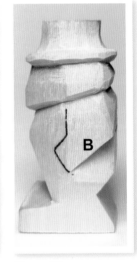

Figure 25

Figure 26

Figure 27

You can see the cuts that are necessary to carve the front portion of the arms in **Fig. 28.** Start at the elbow. Push the point of your knife blade into the wood about ⅛ in. (3 mm) deep and cut down to the pocket line. The cut becomes more shallow as it nears the pocket. It should barely touch the pocket line. Invert the character and thrust the point of your blade about ⅛ in. (3 mm) deep into the wood at the elbow and cut toward the shoulder. The upper end of the cut should be about 1⁄16 in. (1.5 mm) deep. Take out the wood from in front of the A/D line by making a little swinging cut that is shallow at the bottom (point A), goes deep in the middle (the elbow area), then becomes shallow again at the upper end (point D).

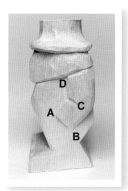

Figure 28

At the top of the A/D line there is an abnormality. The inner armpit does not go as high as the one pictured in **Fig. 28.** To correct this, make a little slicing cut across the D area and remove the excess wood. Compare D in **Fig. 28** with the same area in **Fig. 29.** Cut out this wood on each side.

Step 8: Putting the Hands in the Pockets

Figure 29

Start the process by making a shallow cut with the point of your knife blade straight into the wood at the pocket line. This cut is pictured in **Fig. 28.** It starts 1⁄16 in. (1.5 mm) in front of the arm (point A) and extends 1⁄16 in. (1.5 mm) beyond the arm (point B). This cut leaves a tiny wedge of wood at points A and B on the illustration that needs to be removed. Take out these wedges. From a point about ¼–⅜ in. (6–10 mm) above the pocket cut, lightly shave the wood down toward the pocket. When this is done the hands will appear to be in the pockets.

Step 9: Completing the Arms and Shoulders

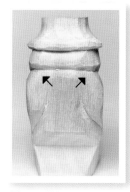

Figure 30

To shape the inner portion of the arm, start by making a V-notch at the juncture where the arm bends (C in **Fig. 28**). Now round the inner arm portion by cutting

Figure 31

Figure 32

Figure 33

Figure 34

toward the notch. When this is accomplished, round the backside of the arms.

Compare **Figs. 27** and **30.** Note the upper arm and shoulder sections. In **Fig. 27** the shoulders are square and the upper arm portion is as wide as the shoulders, even though the arms have been slightly rounded.

In **Fig. 30** the width at the shoulder is slightly less than the width at the elbows. I do this because it makes the character more appealing in my estimation. Also note that the shoulders in **Fig. 30** slope downward whereas in **Fig. 27** there is very little slope. Please make the cuts that you deem necessary to make your character look like the one in **Fig. 30,** but don't overdo these cuts. Actually, very little wood is removed in this whole step.

Step 10: Separating the Hair from the Face

Observe the line drawn on the head of the individual in **Fig. 31.** The mark denotes where you will make a notch cut that will separate the face from the hair. In our Basic Man everything behind this cut will be hair; everything in front of it will be face. Even when you carve ears on a person, this cut is necessary.

In **Fig. 32** the V-cut that separates the hair and face has been made. Near the end of this cut, lines have been drawn to indicate where additional cuts will be made.

Make straight-in stop cuts on these lines similar to those shown in **Fig. 33.** The forward cut defines the jawline and the rear cut designates the bottom of the hair. Remove the triangular piece of wood that is between these cuts and compare your guy with the one in **Fig. 33.**

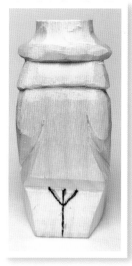

Figure 35

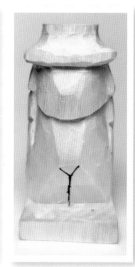

Figure 36

When you made the V-cuts that separated the face from the hair, two ridges were left on the face side. Remove these ridges. When this is done the face will be smaller, will be smooth, and will slant backward from the most forward part of the face to the hairline. Your character's face should look like the one in **Fig. 34.**

Step 11: Dividing the Legs

In this step we divide the legs and shape the shoes. In **Figs. 33** and **34** you can see that the shoes have been shaped somewhat. The toe area has been rounded and cut down a bit and the sides of the shoes have also been rounded.

In **Fig. 35** there is a line drawn from the bottom of the buttocks to the bottom of the figure. There is a small triangle drawn at the top of this line.

Another line is evident in **Fig. 36.** This shows where you will cut when you divide

Figure 37

Figure 38

the legs. Again, a small triangle of wood has been drawn at the top of the line.

Examine **Figs. 37** and **38.** This is the way you want your character to look after you divide the legs.

| Figure 39 | Figure 40 | Figure 41 |

Start the leg division process at the rear of the subject. Stick the point of your blade rather deeply into the wood at the top of the pencil line. Leave the point of the blade in the wood and draw the blade downward toward the bottom of the carving. The blade should go into the wood ⅛–³⁄₁₆ in. (3-5 mm) (Some people wince when they make this cut). Cut out the little triangular piece of wood that you drew at the top of the line. Try to do this in three cuts.

Now move out ¹⁄₁₆ in. (1.5 mm) or so to the right of this long cut and cut in toward the bottom of the first cut. Make the same cut on the left side. Repeat these cuts and compare the way your guy looks to the one in **Fig. 37.**

At the front side of the person you will divide the legs in a similar manner. However, you must separate the shoes before you can disjoin the legs.

The first step is to cut a small wedge of wood from between the big toes. **Fig. 39** shows this cut from the bottom of the shoe.

Do not try to accomplish this feat by doing it in two cuts. Instead, gently push your knife about ⅛ in. (3 mm) into the wood on the centerline. Move out from this cut about ¹⁄₁₆ in. (1.5 mm) and cut toward the first cut. Do this on the other side. Repeat this process on alternate sides until you have removed a wedge of wood the size of the one in **Fig. 39.**

In **Fig. 40** some wood has been cut from the inside of the right shoe. Cuts such as these must be made in order to shape the inner portion of the shoes.

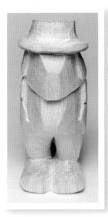

Figure 42   Figure 43   Figure 44   Figure 45

The best way to make this cut is to turn the guy so he is belly-up in your hand with the feet facing away from you. Make a straight cut into the wood at the angle pictured in the illustration. Duplicate this cut on the opposite shoe. Now free this wedge of wood by making a third cut from above the first two. The shoes should look like the ones in **Fig. 41.**

Divide the legs in front the same way you did the legs in the back with one exception: the triangle at the top of the division line in front angles slightly upward.

When your character's legs are divided, check **Figs. 37** and **38.** This is the way you want them to look.

Step 12: Separating the Legs

In step 11 you learned how to divide the legs. An optional leg treatment is pictured in **Figs. 42** and **43.** This is the way my standard carvings look now. The legs are separated but the shoes are together. This look is more difficult to achieve but is well worth the effort. With the legs separated the carving has more appeal and is, therefore, more valuable.

Figure 46   Figure 47   Figure 48

I can't tell you how to attain this look. You just have to dig around between the legs until you accomplish the results you seek. You will need a skinny blade and a small V-gouge. Try to achieve as smooth a look as you can on the inner leg portion then use the V-gouge to clean out the area between the shoes. **Do not separate the shoes.** Leave some wood so the shoes will be connected.

Step 13: Carving the Bottom of the Pants

Fig. 44 shows where the bottom of the pants should be if you separated the legs. Draw these lines on your carving then remove the line with a small V-gouge. If the V-cuts are not sharp enough, cut away the fuzzies with your knife.

If you divided the pants but did not separate them, the line drawn on the figure in **Fig. 45** is where you want to carve the bottoms of the pants.

Step 14: Finishing the Shoes

The action required in this step is relatively easy. It requires two cuts to carve each heel and a little V-gouge work to cut the soles.

Examples of how the completed heels look are pictured in **Figs. 46** and **47**. **Fig. 46** shows the heel from the right side and **Fig. 47** is a view from below.

Start the process by drawing a ⅛–³⁄₁₆ in. (3-5 mm) line on the bottom of each shoe that is ³⁄₁₆–¼ in. (5-6 mm) from, and parallel to, the rear of the figure. The lines start at the outside edges of the shoes and go inward.

On each line make a stop cut straight into the wood. The cut should be ⅛ in. (3 mm) deep at the outside edge of the line and should be continuously less deep until it has no depth at the inner end of the line.

From ⅛ in. (3 mm) in front of this cut, make a second cut that slants into, and is the same depth as, the first cut. If the two cuts are of the same depth, a small wedge of wood will pop out. When this happens on one side, duplicate the cuts on the other.

To finish this step, draw a line around the shoes where the soles should be located and take out this line with your small V-tool. When this is done, compare your character with the ones in **Figs. 48** and **49.** If you are satisfied with the looks, the shoes are complete.

Check out **Figs. 50** and **51** for a different shoe look. Here, the toes have been turned up a bit. To attain this result, cut out a portion of the underside of the front edge of the shoes and hollow out some of the upper portions of the shoes between the toes and the pant legs. Do this very carefully. With the toes turned up, the heels are unchanged, but the soles must be cut with a little "upsweep" at the toes.

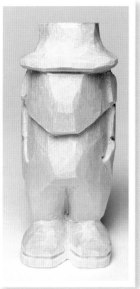

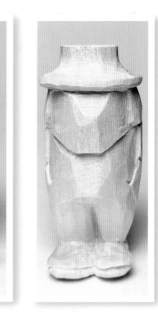

Figure 49   Figure 50   Figure 51

| Figure 52 | Figure 53 | Figure 54 |

Another shoe that I enjoy carving is depicted in **Figs. 52, 53,** and **54.** It's my version of the tennis shoe. They are easy to carve because they have no heels and all the cuts are made with a small V-tool.

Start this process by drawing a line around each shoe that is ¹⁄₁₆ in. (1.5 mm) from the bottom of the piece. Remove this line by cutting along it with a V-gouge. Now make a series of perpendicular cuts that starts at the sole line and go past the bottom of the shoe. Mark a line on each foot that goes over the toe area to represent the toecap. Cut these lines away with a V-gouge and your character is ready to run.

Step 15: Dressing Your Guy

I told you in the beginning that the guy you would carve first would be a simple fellow. Simple, in this case, meaning uncomplicated rather than stupid.

Your faceless character should be complete now except for his attire. The easiest way to clothe him is to make him look like the fellow in **Figs. 52, 53,** and **54.** That guy has on pants and a sweater (or T-shirt) worn outside his pants.

Start the clothing process by drawing a line similar to the one in the illustrations around the middle of your person. Now cut ¹⁄₁₆ in. (1.5 mm) deep into the wood on this line with your V-gouge. If the V-cuts are too indistinct, sharpen the cuts with your knife.

Your Basic Man is now complete except he has no face. In the next section I'll show you how to carve a simple face so you can complete your character.

CARVING THE FACE

If you completed the exercise in Carving the Body you now have a neat carving of a character without a face. This section is designed to teach you how to carve a face for that character.

Many of the inexperienced character carvers I have taught in workshops get weak in the knees when told to carve a face on their character. They are intimidated by the complexity of the face. Many have experienced disaster in the past when trying to carve eyes; others have found carving mouths equally difficult. Several have admitted they have no idea how to make the nose look like it belongs with the face. The face that I teach is very simple and one that most people can learn to carve well after a little instruction and a bit of practice. If you carefully follow the directions that are detailed in this section, you will find that carving faces is not as difficult as you thought.

Let's start the learning process by carving a practice face stick. Look at **Figs. 55** and **56.** Cut several blank practice sticks like these out of 1 in. (25 mm) basswood. The dimensions of the blank sticks are ¹³⁄₁₆ × ¹³⁄₁₆ × 3 in. (21 × 21 × 76 mm).

To shape the practice stick, follow these directions:

Figure 55

1. From the top of the stick, measure 1 in. (25 mm) toward the center and draw a line around the piece at this distance.
2. Draw a similar line 1 in. (25 mm) from the bottom that circles the block. The stick is now divided into three equal parts.
3. At each corner of the block, mark a line that is ½ in. (13 mm) from the top (line A in the illustration). Make another mark at each corner that is ½ in. (13 mm) from the bottom of the stick. This is line B on the example.

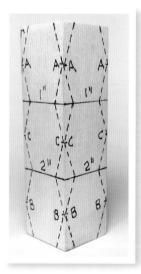

Figure 56

4. Draw another short line at each corner that is 1½ in. (38 mm) from the top. This is line C in the picture.
5. From each A mark, take out the wood between dash lines at the top of the stick. Do this by making straight cuts that start at the A marks and angle inward about ⅛ in. (3 mm) toward the top.
6. Make like cuts at the bottom of the stick. These cuts start at the B mark and extend through the bottom of the stick.
7. Remove the wood from the A mark to the 1 in. (25 mm) line and from the C mark to the 1 in. (25 mm) line. These cuts should meet at the 1 in. (25 mm) line. Where the lines meet, the cut should be about ⅛ in. (3 mm) deep and no more than ¼ in. (6 mm) wide.
8. Make the same cuts from the C mark to the 2 in. (51 mm) line and from the B mark to the 2 in. (51 mm) line.
9. Your stick should look like **Fig. 57.**

In **Fig. 58** the numbers 1, 2, and 3 have been written on one edge. Mark these numbers on your stick then rotate the stick a quarter turn to the left. Write 4, 5, and 6 on the stick as indicated in **Fig. 59.** Rotate the stick another quarter turn and write 7, 8, and 9 at the appropriate places. Make one more turn and mark this edge 10, 11, and 12.

Figure 57

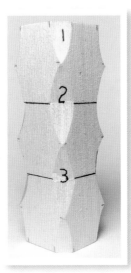

Figure 58

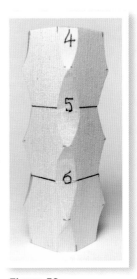

Figure 59

Carving the Practice Stick

In the space under each of the twelve numbers a portion of a face will be carved. The high point in each space represents the tip of the nose.

Please study **Figs. 60–63.** The cuts you will make to carve a face are depicted in these illustrations. Before you make a cut, look at the appropriate illustration, read the text that describes the action, and then make the cut(s).

As you studied the illustrations you probably observed that the action is cumulative. Each step builds on the next. What is on one step must first be on the ensuing one if you are to make the new cuts successfully.

As an example, the step 1 cut (the brow cut) must be made on step 2 before the eye cuts can be made. Step 3 has a brow cut and eye cuts plus the nose cut. Step 4 has all of the above plus an additional cut.

As you carve the stick you will become proficient at making some of the cuts. Carve several sticks, and face carving will become routine. When this happens stay with the system but experiment with the features and create new and more interesting faces.

The Steps

1. The Brow Cut. This is a V-cut that is made where the top of the nose meets the bottom of the forehead. The cut is about ³⁄₁₆ in. (5 mm) long and ¹⁄₁₆ in. (1.5 mm) deep.

2. The Eye Cuts. Be sure to make a brow cut in the second space, then make two eye cuts. The eye cuts are V-cuts that are the same size as the brow cut. The cuts start at the midpoint of the brow cut and angle slightly downward.

3. The Nose Cut. Make another brow cut, another set of eye cuts, and a straight-in cut where you think the bottom of the nose should be located. Take out the wood under the nose.

Figure 60

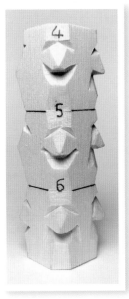

Figure 61

4. The Clip Cut. Cut off the outside portions of the nose cut. Do this by first making straight-in cuts that are about 30 degrees from horizontal. Complete the cuts by turning your knife blade on its side and cutting away the wood that is between the outer portion of the nose cut and the straight-in cuts that were just made.

5. The Triangle Cut. This is one of the most important facial cuts you will make. It is a big first step in making the nose a part of the face rather than just a lump of wood sticking out from the middle of the face space.

You will make three small cuts on each side of the nose in the space where you removed wood at step 4. The three cuts form a triangle with the top of the triangle toward the top of the stick.

Stick the point of your knife blade straight into the wood that is alongside the nose. The cut is approximately ⅛ in. (3 mm) deep and as long. This is the first leg of an equilateral triangular cut.

The second leg of the triangle should duplicate the first cut, but it should start at the top of the first cut and angle away from the nose toward the outer part of the face. Together, the two cuts should look like this: **/**

The third cut, the base cut, is made straight across the space between the bottoms of the other two cuts. When you make this cut, a small triangle-shaped piece of wood should pop out. When this step is complete, there should be a small triangular hole at each side of the nose. Recheck the illustration. Your cuts must be similar to the ones in the illustration.

6. The Cheek Furrow Cut. On either side of the nose most of us have grooves that start at the outside edges of the bottom of the nose and extend downward toward the jaw. Dr. Dave Dunham, who is an orthodontist and famous caricature carver, calls these lines *nasolabial grooves*. My friend Pete LeClair, another noted caricature carver, calls these grooves "expression lines."

Whatever you call them, they determine to a great extent the temperament of your character. If the lines go straight downward, the face will have a grumpy look. If the lines angle slightly toward the outside of the face, the character's expression will be more pleasant. If the lines at the bottom are wide apart, the person appears to be a happy camper.

To make this cut, make a stop cut with the point of your blade that is ¼ in. (6 mm) long and curves outward and downward from the nose triangle (step 5). The depth of this cut should be ¹⁄₁₆ in. (1.5 mm) deep at the top and more shallow at the terminus of the cut.

The second part of the cut is made by laying your blade flat against the wood on the mouth side of the previous cut and making a flat cut into the stop cut. When you have completed these cuts on each side of the face, you will have established a slight mound where the mouth will be carved.

7. Smoothing the Mouth Mound. If you made the cuts correctly in step 6 you left two small ridges on the mouth mound. Remove these ridges and you will have a smooth surface when you carve the mouth later.

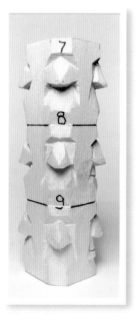

8. Shaping the Nose. The nose is shaped in steps 8 and 9. Begin the process by making a dot on each side of the nose at the brow line that is ¹⁄₁₆ in. (1.5 mm) from the center of the nose. The distance between the dots is equivalent to the width of an eye. Draw a line from each triangle cut (step 5) to the dot on the same side of the nose.

With the edge of your blade, make a cut straight into the wood on this line. The depth of the cut should be the same as the depth of the eye cuts (step 2).

Turn your knife blade on its side and make a flat cut into the stop cut you just made. This cut starts at the outer limit of the eye cut (step 2). Do this on the opposite side of the nose and the step is complete.

Figure 62

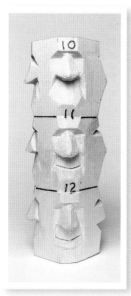

Figure 63

9. More Nose Shaping. Two more cuts are necessary before the nose looks right. Near the bottom of the nose is a bit of fibro-fatty tissue that gives it additional shape. Some people call these protrusions "nose wings." Others refer to the area as the outer nostril area.

To achieve the right look, make a shallow cut into the wood where you think the top of the wing should be, then swing the point of the blade up toward the inside of the eye cut. After you make the same cut on the other side of the nose, the step is complete.

10. Eye Cuts II. When the nose was shaped the eyes were destroyed. They must be recut. Do this by making V-cuts where the eyes had previously been. These cuts should be a bit deeper than the first eye cuts and slant down very slightly or not at all. I prefer a little slant.

11. The Mouth Cut. Draw a line across the mouth mound where you want the mouth to be located. Extend the line from one cheek furrow to the other. With a sharp ⅛ in. (3 mm) V-gouge, cut into this line.

Because V-gouge cuts are not as sharp as I like them to be, I deepen them slightly with my knife. If you make a tiny V-cut on the mouth line, the mouth looks much more distinct.

12. The Lower Lip. At this point the lower lip of your practice-stick face is probably sticking out much farther than the upper lip. The face has a "pooch-mouth" look. Cut the lower lip back a bit so it will be less prominent than the upper lip.

The lower lip in most *Homo sapiens* is shorter than the upper lip. To achieve this effect cut from each side of the lower lip a little triangle of wood at the point where the lip connects with the cheek furrows.

The lower lip can be cut with a knife or a U-gouge. If you use a knife, your first cut will be made at the center of the bottom lip. Position the knife blade so it is pointed straight into the wood 1/16 in. (1.5 mm) below the mouth cut. Cut into the wood 1/16 in. (1.5 mm) and roll the blade downward.

Move your blade to the left a bit and make the same type of cut. The last cut on this side should extend into the corner of the mouth. This cut rolls down as before, but must then be rolled slightly to the left in order to clean out the wood from the corner where the mouth meets the cheek furrow.

The opposite side of the lip is cut in much the same manner except the last cut will be down and right instead of down and left. I invert the stick when I make the cuts on this side of the face.

If you use a U-gouge to carve the lower lip, cut out the wood below the center of the lip first. The next cuts start at the juncture of the mouth and the cheek furrows. These cuts curve downward and angle toward the center cut. When the lines are joined the lower lip should look like the one in the illustration.

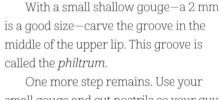

With a small shallow gouge—a 2 mm is a good size—carve the groove in the middle of the upper lip. This groove is called the *philtrum*.

One more step remains. Use your small gouge and cut nostrils so your guy can breathe. Don't cut too deeply or you'll break the nose off.

Compare your face stick with the illustrations. If your piece looks like the dog chewed it, reread the directions, study the examples carefully, and carve another practice stick. If the comparison is favorable, however, you are ready to carve a face on your character.

Brother Gasper

Before you start that process I'd like to pass on one more bit of information. You want your characters to look like they are wearing their hats. To achieve this look make all brow cuts and all eye cuts as close to the brim as possible.

You now have all the information you need to carve a face. Carve a great one on your character. Good luck!!!!

Face over Body

The face is the key to carving a character that people "ooh" and "aah" over. If you carve a character with a great face and a so-so body it will still be regarded as a Good Carving. If the REVERSE is true, however—a great body but a so-so face—that character will have little, if any, appeal.

Happy and Hairy

Happy faces are more popular than grumpy ones, and characters with facial hair are popular.

Gilbert

DRESSING THE CHARACTER

The simplest way to dress the Basic Man was described in section one. He can be dressed many other ways without altering the pattern. Other interesting alternative costumes can be carved with only slight variation of the pattern. Try some of the combinations listed below.

1. In overalls with a farmer-style hat.
2. In overalls with a hardhat.
3. In shirt, pants, and tie.
4. In shirt, pants, and no tie.
5. In shirt, pants and vest, tie or tieless.
6. In shorts with socks of varying lengths. One sock up and one sock down. Shoed or shoeless. Hole in sock with toes poking through.
7. In shorts and a muscle shirt or T-shirt.
8. In a tank top and pants.
9. With one side of his shirt tucked in his belt and the other side outside the belt.
10. In a sailor suit, clown suit, or like a Keystone Kop.
11. In shirt, pants or a coat too small or too large for him.
12. With holes and tears in his clothing.
13. With frayed or patched clothes.
14. Wearing suspenders.
15. In long underwear.
16. In a doctor-type coat.
17. Like a Boy Scout.
18. In hillbilly garb.
19. Wearing a headband or a cap instead of a hat.
20. With his pants tucked in his boots.
21. In various types of shoes and boots.
22. With one shoe on and one shoe off.
23. With holes in his shoes.
24. Barefooted.
25. As a caveman with a one-piece suit.
26. In a loincloth.
27. With hair only.
28. In very wrinkled clothing.
29. In army combat gear.

30. Wearing a flight jacket and an aviation helmet.
31. Dressed like a cold-weather rancher in a lambskin-trimmed jacket.
32. Wearing a bowtie or an extra-long tie.
33. In a toga or robe, like an ancient Roman, friar, or wizard might wear.
34. In a sweater and knickers.
35. As a logger or a skier wearing a stocking cap.
36. In an old-timey swimsuit with a hole in the knee.
37. In an apron and chef's hat.
38. With something in his back pocket.
39. In a long coat like a flasher might wear.
40. Wearing the uniform of a Civil War soldier.

You can change the Basic Man in other ways:

1. Carve him thinner or fatter than the pattern.
2. Add facial hair.
3. Make him bald or semi-bald.
4. Carve him with hair over one or both eyes.
5. Change his hairstyle. Part his hair in the middle or give him a flattop, an Afro, or make his hair curly.
6. Make him pigeon-toed or knock-kneed.
7. Bow his legs.
8. Carve him fat with skinny legs.
9. Give him an extra-large buttocks.
10. Make him very thin but with a potbelly.
11. Have one foot slightly overlap part of the other.

Radolf

The idea I'm suggesting here is that your characters do not have to look alike. After you become familiar with character carving, try to make each carving different from the others you have done.

I usually start carving a character with something specific in mind and end up with a person that is entirely different. As I make cuts, especially on the face, I often see a personality emerging. Generally, I go with the flow and wind up with a character that is more interesting than the one I had originally contemplated.

When you carve these little guys, start with an idea of what you want to achieve but be flexible enough to change. Sometimes the character in the wood does not want to be what you want him to be. If you expect him to be a farmer and he sees himself as a brain surgeon, try to find a middle ground, or carve him as he wants to be.

The next section of the book, Carving 201, will explain other ways to enhance the Basic Man. I hope you will carve several characters from the Basic Man pattern before you move to the advanced section.

PAINTING THE CHARACTER

A good carving can be greatly enhanced by a good paint job. Conversely, a good carving can be ruined by an inferior finish. Look around at any carving show and you will see examples of each.

I think most good carvers will agree that a quality finish is one that allows the wood grain to show through the paint or stain. A bad finish is one that is applied too thickly. It should be apparent, by observation alone, that the object was carved from wood.

Most of the people who author carving books have a preferred method of finishing their carvings. Over the years I've tried most of the systems that others have espoused. None proved satisfactory until I discovered those marvelous ready-mixed acrylic paints that are packaged in 2 oz. (59 mL) plastic squeeze bottles.

This product is sold in most arts-and-crafts stores. Some of the more common brand names are Ceramcoat by Delta, Folk Art and Apple Barrel colors by Plaid Enterprises, Accent by Illinois Bronze Paint Company, and Americana by Decco Art. Some of the carvers that I know prefer one brand over the others but I don't find much difference between them.

If you shop around a little bit you can find just about any color you can imagine. Instead of colors like red, black, or green, you'll find bluebell, hippo grey, denim blue, pine needle green, harvest gold, dark chocolate, and molasses. Each brand offers about the same assortment of colors but the names of the colors are different from brand to brand. Even the skin tones have different names.

If you have not settled on a system for painting your characters, you might want to give the method described below a try. It's not very complicated or costly.

Buy a few bottles of paint and practice painting on a scrap piece of wood. To start you will want a white, a black, a red, a blue, and a skin tone.

You'll need five brushes: a #1 flat, a #3 tapered, a #1 tapered, a O tapered, and a OO tapered. Buy good brushes and clean them thoroughly after each use. They will last a long time if you care for them properly.

When you mix your paint use one drop of color to five drops of water. If it's too dark, add a little water. With white paint, use one drop of paint to four drops of water. You'll have to experiment and find what works for you.

Harold Enlow advises his students to brush some mixed paint on a sheet of newspaper in order to determine if the mixture is right. If the newspaper print can't be read through the paint, the blend is too thick. That's good advice from an expert.

Painting basswood is very similar to painting a blotter: it soaks up paint fast and spreads out. The tendency is to overload your brush with paint so you can complete the job fast. Don't do this. An overloaded brush will spread paint where you don't want it to go.

When you paint your Basic Man do not paint two parts that are adjacent to each other if you are using different colors on the two parts. Paint the hat, the shirt, and the shoes. Let these dry then paint the hair and pants. When these dry, paint the skin.

After the flesh color dries you are ready to paint the eyes. Moisten your O or OO brush with water, then dip it in full-strength white paint and fill the eye groove with paint. Do the same for the other eye and let this dry. When sufficient time has elapsed, paint a dab of blue, black, or brown paint in each eye to complete the painting process.

When the painting is done and the piece is dry, one more step remains. Mix one part of boiled linseed oil with one part turpentine. If you can find a turpentine substitute like Turpenoid use it instead of regular turpentine. It doesn't have the strong turpentine odor.

Dunk your character in this mixture for a couple of seconds, pull him out, and blot him with a paper towel. This last step is the coup de grace—the finishing touch. It softens the colors, seals the wood, brings out the grain, and gives the carving a bit of sheen.

Now, a word of caution. The paper towels that were used to blot your character may become hazardous material. They can cause spontaneous combustion if improperly processed. I suggest that you store these used materials in a sealed can of water until you can dispose of them.

I have one more suggestion. Encourage your partner or spouse to learn to paint. If he or she becomes a better painter than you are, it will benefit both of you. Your significant other will find great satisfaction in being an integral part of your success and you will be able to do what you like best—carve.

CARVING A MORE COMPLEX CHARACTER

CARVING EARS

In this section we will alter the appearance of the Basic Man by uncovering his ears. Although he looks OK with hair covering his ears, he will look more complete if his ears show.

Realistic ears are pretty standard. They all have the same parts and the same basic shape. Usually we don't notice the appearance of people's ears unless they deviate greatly from the norm. Ears don't express character unless they are distorted in some way.

They may be carved larger or smaller than ordinary, they may stick out from the head, or they may be cauliflowered. Other than those abnormalities, ears are just ears.

The basic ear resembles a C with the bottom part skewed slightly forward. Ordinarily the upper part is larger than the bottom section. The ear that I carve has the C shape but none of the parts that are inside the realistic ear are carved.

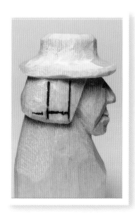

Figure 64

Start the process by carving a head like the Basic Man. On the head draw the lines that you see in **Fig. 64.** The ear will be carved from the space within the lines.

The vertical line closest to the ear is drawn in the middle of the head. The rear line is about ³⁄₁₆ in. (5 mm). behind the forward line. The horizontal line denotes the bottom of the ear. It is drawn in line with the bottom of the nose. The ear extends upward from this line to the hat brim. If the character was not wearing a hat the upper horizontal line would be drawn at eyebrow level.

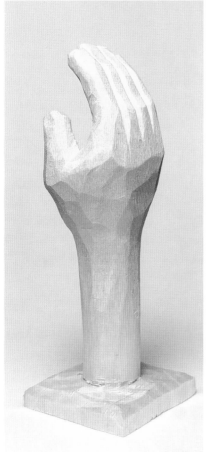

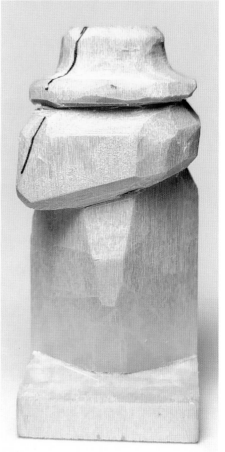

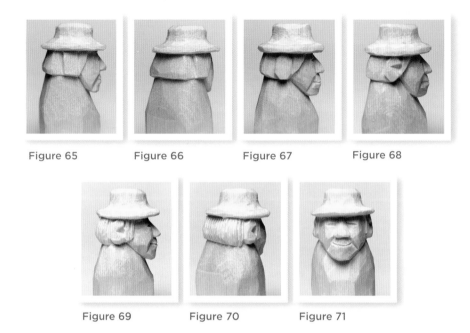

Figure 65   Figure 66   Figure 67   Figure 68

Figure 69   Figure 70   Figure 71

In **Fig. 65** the first ear cuts are portrayed. The cut on the front line is a thin, fairly deep V-cut that separates the ear from the sideburns. The rear cut goes straight into the wood about ⅟₁₆ in. (1.5 mm) and the wood behind this cut is removed. **Fig. 66** shows the depth of the cut and the amount of wood that was cut away.

In **Fig. 67** the corners of the ear have been notched. A small triangle of wood was cut from each corner.

The next cut is an important one that is difficult to portray. The back part of the ear usually stands out farther from the head than the forward portion does. To create this look, make a flat cut from the rear of the ear to the sideburn that angles inward about ⅟₁₆ in. (1.5 mm) The result of this cut is shown in **Figs. 67** and **68.**

Make a notch cut in the middle of the forward edge of the ear similar to the cut in **Fig. 68.** If you slightly hollow the inside of the ear it will resemble the one in **Fig. 69.** This action makes the ear look a little more realistic.

Fig. 69 also shows how the ear looks when the hair has been carved and when the back of the jaw angles upward into the front of the ear.

A rear view of the complete ear is pictured in **Fig. 70.** The front view, showing both ears, is depicted in **Fig. 71.**

HAIR DOS AND DON'TS

Billions of dollars each year are spent on hair care products. People who are concerned with their looks gladly spend the time and money it requires to keep their hair well groomed and appropriate to their perception of themselves.

To a great extent hair defines character. A clown is expected to have some type of preposterous hair. An old man is expected to be bald, semi-bald, or have thinning hair. Goofy-looking people should have goofy hair.

A doctor, lawyer, preacher, or banker with strange hair is suspect. Do you want to deal with a banker that has clown-type hair? Would you like to be treated by a pink-haired doctor? I don't think so: you wouldn't trust them.

It follows, then, that the people you carve should have hair that is appropriate to their character or status in life. If your person is to have some special hairdo you should plan his hair in advance. If it deviates from the ordinary it won't just happen. Experiment with some of these hairdos:

1. Bald or semi-bald
2. Wild and wooly
3. Over eye(s)
4. Curly
5. Afro
6. Flattop
7. With long, short, or no sideburns
8. Fluffed out at the sides
9. Long in the back
10. With only a tuft on top

Examples of several hairdos are pictured in the illustrations in the Rogues' Gallery.

Hair is usually carved with a V-gouge or a U-gouge. With small characters the ⅛ in. (3 mm) size works best. A V-gouge is used when cutting individual strands of hair and the U-gouge creates the impression of carved hair without carving each strand separately. Curly hair is often carved with a U-gouge.

Generally, hair does not hang down in a straight, continuous line from top to bottom. Some hairs do hang this way but most angle right or left or curl one way then another.

For several reasons normal hair has a tendency to stick together. When several individual hairs cling together a cluster is formed, and like individual strands, clusters seldom fall straight downward.

You can achieve the cluster look by cutting valleys into the hair area with a V-gouge, U-gouge, or a knife before carving individual strands of hair. Clusters can also be formed by varying the depths of the V-gouge cuts as you carve individual hairs.

Another hair peculiarity is that hair is not necessarily the same length all over the head. When small characters are carved it is difficult to vary hair length because the area where the hair is to be carved is so limited.

In an attempt to create the impression that the hair on my character's head is not all the same length I usually carve the bottom part of the hair first and carve the upper portion second. The bottom part is carved with short overlapping strokes that angle downward. The upper portion is carved with short upward strokes that overlap occasionally.

After the hair is carved I often cut little wedges out of the wood at the bottom of the hairline. This makes the hair appear even more uneven.

Facial Hair

Soon after I began to concentrate on carving characters I noticed that people bought the guys with facial hair more often than they purchased the smooth-shaven ones. I don't know if this is true with other character carvers, but the trend for me has not changed over the years.

People seem to be somewhat fascinated by facial hair. Perhaps it's because a person with hair on his face is less ordinary than one without hair. It might even be the Santa Claus influence. Would Santa be as loved or as cuddly without a mustache and full beard?

Harold, Antonio, and Wayne

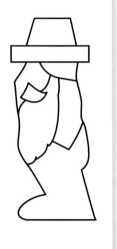

Even a little facial hair is noticeable; a heavy mustache and/or beard really stands out. It's even more stunning if the person is female . . .

If you want to shock your friends and acquaintances, either grow some facial hair if you don't wear any, or shave off what you normally wear. It will not go unnoticed.

Facial hair is not difficult to carve but it must be planned in advance. In the pattern at the left there is ample room for any type of facial hair. Decide in advance what type of hair you want your character to wear and block it off early in the carving process.

Facial hair styles that you can carve from this pattern include:

1. Long, full beard with mustache
2. Short beard and mustache
3. Mustache only
4. Beard only
5. Goatee
6. Fu Manchu mustache (long thin one that hangs down)
7. Muttonchops
8. Walrus-style mustache
9. A heavy stubble

Examples of different hairdos and facial hair styles are pictured in the illustrations in the Rogues Gallery.

Mustaches

A mustache should start at the triangular cut and can be carved with the ends swooped up or turned down. The up-swoop also allows room for a lip. Study the examples, and how the facial hair DEFINES the character.

GRINS AND GRIMACES, GNAWERS AND GNASHERS

The mouth is the most mobile part of the face. Because of its mobility it can show a wide range of expressions with only the help of the cheek furrows.

When the mouth turns up it indicates happiness; turned down it expresses sorrow and suffering. When open, the mouth shows fear, surprise, anger, and yelling. A small mouth carved straight across implies boredom or indifference.

The expressions generated by the mouth are greatly enhanced when the other facial features get into the act. The whole face is involved when human beings express extreme emotion. The eyes and the eyebrows are major contributors; the forehead and even the nose participate when we emote big time.

Look in the mirror and try to register these emotions: laughter, anger, and pain. What facial part is involved the most when you express these feelings? For me it's the mouth.

The Mouth Mound

When you carved the face on your character you created a mouth mound when you carved the cheek furrows in step 6. You smoothed the mound in step 7, carved the mouth in step 11, and added a lip in step 12.

The mouth mound you created is convex in shape. The corners sink into the face more so than in the middle of the mouth. This convexity makes it possible to carve teeth that look sorta human.

Wise Riven

Tooth Info

Before I started to write this discourse on teeth I decided to consult my good friend and tooth guru Dr. Dave Dunham, orthodontist, superb caricature carver, caricaturist, humorist, and a bunch of other good things. His words of wisdom are quoted verbatim below.

People have thirty-two permanent teeth, sixteen uppers, sixteen lowers (counting wisdom teeth). Each arch of sixteen is arranged in a horseshoe, or half-circle shape, with the upper arch on a larger radius than the lower. The upper teeth, therefore, fit *outside* the lowers when the teeth are closed together.

The jaws themselves are arranged in a half-circle also, but on a larger radius than the teeth. When a person smiles the *corners* of the mouth are stretched laterally around the jaw curvature. The *lips* are stretched tightly against the front teeth, but the back teeth, being on a smaller curvature, recede in toward the midline of the body, thus creating a space at the corners of the mouth between themselves and the cheeks.

When carving teeth it is cosmetically better to show only a few teeth than too many. The teeth need to be disproportionate on the **large** side. It is best to show six teeth at most, even on a large, wide smile.

Make sure the teeth are *behind* the lips, and that there is space in the corners of the mouth.

When carving female faces, leave the teeth together as a unit—do not show individual tooth separations. For some reason, individually carved teeth detract from the aesthetics of a female face whereas the arch as a unit enhances its prettiness.

I'd like to re-emphasize five things that David says:

1. Each arch of sixteen teeth is arranged in a horseshoe or half-circle shape.
2. The upper arch fits outside the lower when the teeth are closed together.
3. It's better to show only a few teeth than too many.
4. The teeth must be carved behind the lips.
5. There must be space in the corners of the mouth between the cheek and the teeth.

The Shape of Teeth

According to the tooth pundit, the incisors, the four teeth in the center of the upper arch, are shaped like snow shovels. The lower incisors, because they are smaller, are shaped like sharpshooter shovels. All canines, the teeth on the outside of the incisors, are shaped like diamonds.

Carving Teeth

Before you begin to carve teeth, examine the character's mouth mound and cheek furrows. Is the mound smooth and is it convex ? Are the cheek furrows carved correctly for the mood you plan to portray? If the answers to these questions are affirmative, you are ready to do a little dental work.

Carving Teeth in a Smiling Face

Draw a mouth on your character's face. When you do so keep in mind that the lips are stretched tightly against the front teeth when a person smiles. For this reason the upper lip is usually drawn straight across the mouth mound from one cheek furrow to the other.

The bottom lip is a curved line and this curvature produces a smile when the lips are parted. The distance between the lips determines how happy the person appears. A slight separation expresses happiness; a wide-open mouth indicates hilarity.

On the top mouth line make a cut from one cheek furrow to the other that goes straight into the wood 1/16 in. (1.5 mm) deep. Make the same type of cut on the bottom line. You have just made two rather long stop cuts.

Dough

The next step is to remove a sliver of wood from the wood inside the mouth area that is adjacent to the stop cuts. These cuts delineate the upper and lower limits of the teeth.

At this point I like to cut the teeth back slightly more at the top so they will angle outward a bit from top to bottom. This action ensures that the teeth will be behind the upper lip.

With your skinny-blade knife, cut deeply into each corner of the mouth and take out a small triangle of wood. You do this because the upper arch is shaped like a horseshoe and these cuts will create that look when the mouth is viewed from the front.

Round the upper and lower lips slightly. If the lower lip is too prominent or if it protrudes beyond the teeth, remove some of the excess wood.

Determine where the bottom of the teeth will be and cut out the wood that is between the bottom of the teeth and the lower lip. Carve a lower lip like the one in step 12 of the face stick (page 49). Make sure that the lower lip is shorter than the upper lip.

Draw in the teeth. On these little guys there is usually only enough room for four snow shovels (incisors). On each "tooth" line make thin V-cuts that are just deep enough to show four separate teeth.

When this is accomplished it will appear that your character's mouth contains six teeth—four distinct incisors and a bit of wood at each corner of the mouth that suggests additional teeth.

When you paint your character, color the teeth white unless he smokes or uses smokeless tobacco. If he is a smoker, a chewer, or a dipper, paint his teeth a yellowish-brown color.

When I paint teeth I dip the tip of my brush in water and then touch the tip to a glob of full-strength paint. This tiny bit of water makes the paint flow better than it would if the brush was dry when dipped in the paint.

HOMEWORK ASSIGNMENT

If you are new to character carving and you're unsure about carving faces and heads, the exercise described below will help you gain experience carving both. Copy these two-headed patterns on poster board and transfer the patterns to several of your 2 in. (51 mm) blocks of wood.

Carve two heads on each piece of wood. Use the carving techniques described earlier in the book but make each head/face unique.

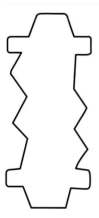 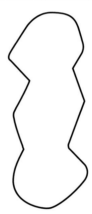

Try some of these suggestions:

1. Carve a different hat on each head.
2. Change hats to caps.
3. Move the cap bills to the side or to the rear of the head.
4. Vary the size of the noses.
5. Move noses and mouths up or down on the face.
6. Carve teeth in some of the mouths.
7. Carve a guy with his tongue hanging out.
8. Modify the hairdos.
9. Duplicate some of the characters in the Rogues' Gallery.

> ## Oh, *bleep*!
> An "Oh! Bleep" cut is not always a bad thing. It can be an opportunity to learn something new or even develop a new character.

This should be a fun exercise for you. Don't worry about making mistakes. You'll learn as much from your mistakes as from your successes.

TURNING THE CHARACTER'S HEAD

One of the most dramatic ways to enhance the Basic Man is to turn his head slightly to one side. When the head of a character is turned, he appears less static than when his head is pointed straight forward. He seems to be in the process of doing something. Turning the head is especially effective in a two-or-more-person scene when the heads are turned toward each other as though they are engaged in conversation.

The turning process is not difficult if you stay alert throughout the process to where the nose is pointed and realize that when one part of the head moves, all the other parts of the head turn the same distance and in the same direction. Be aware also, if this is your first "turning," that the natural tendency is to allow the head to return to the straight position as you go through the process.

When you carved your Basic Man he looked like the person in **Fig. 72** at the conclusion of step 3. Carve one of your blocks of wood to look like the example and I'll show you how to turn his head.

The first step is to draw a line up the right front corner of the block, across the hat, and down the back to the bottom of the hairline. Make a short horizontal mark on the front line that is ½ in. (13 mm) from the bottom of the hat brim. Make a like mark on the back line ¼ to ³⁄₃₂ in. (6 to 2 mm) from the bottom of the hat brim. Connect the front and back marks as you did when you defined the head on the Basic Man. The shoulder line should go straight across the back of your piece. **Figs. 73** and **74** show these lines.

Figure 72

Figure 73

Figure 74

Figure 75

Figure 76

Figure 77

Figure 78

Figure 79

Figure 80

Make a deep V-cut at the bottom of the front vertical line. This cut will separate the chin from the chest. Make additional V-cuts on the "head" line at the back and on each side of the figure. The back cut is directly opposite the chin cut and the side cuts are halfway between the front and rear cuts. These cuts are pictured in **Figs. 75** and **76.**

With your ¼ in. (6 mm) V-tool or your knife, cut into the "head" line to a depth of ¹⁄₁₆ to ³⁄₃₂ in. (1.5 to 2 mm). When this is done your guy should look like the one in **Figs. 77** and **78.**

Please observe in **Fig. 78** that the shoulders of the character are level. When the head on a carving is turned to one side there is a natural inclination to lower the shoulder on the "turned" side and to raise the shoulder on the opposite side. If you square the shoulders at this stage of the carving you can eliminate this problem.

Remove the ridge that the V-cuts created and round the back just below the hairline. You can observe these cuts in **Figs. 79** and **80.**

| Figure 81 | Figure 82 | Figure 83 |

When you shaped the Basic Man you shaped the upper body in step 4 and made the body angular. Follow the procedures described in that step when you shape this guy's body but stop at the head. The end result of these cuts is found in **Fig. 81.**

The facial area is next. It must be carved to resemble the head in **Fig. 82.** If you have any questions about how to do this, refer back to step 5, Defining the Head, on page 30.

The procedures for completing the character are the same as those for carving the Basic Man. The finished product is pictured in **Fig. 83.**

CARVING HANDS

When I decided to include in the book a section on carving hands I researched the carving books that are in my library. I was surprised to find only one with worthwhile information about hands; my search led me next to anatomy books for artists. Many of these books provide a wealth of information about hands. Some provide graphic illustrations that show how the hand works, why it works that way, and how it looks when it is posed in a number of different positions.

An even better source for information about the type of hands that most of us carve can be found in books on cartooning. Jack Hamm, in his book *Cartooning the Head and Figure,* shows eight basic hand positions that he thinks are adequate for most cartoonists. Some cartoonists, he states, do very well with less than eight.

Cartoon hands are usually drawn without knuckles or fingernails, and all the digits resemble small sausages. This is a good description of the hands I carve. The hands of my characters are more childlike than realistic. They are chubby from top to bottom and are devoid of knuckles or fingernails.

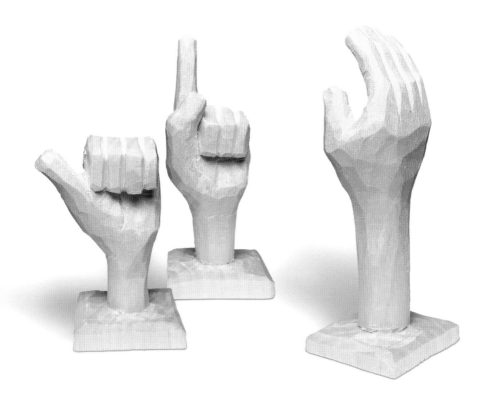

Although the hands described above are not realistic hands, they still look like hands. When people look at your characters you want them to recognize what those things are that are at the ends of the arms.

Carving acceptable hands requires some basic knowledge about hands. The best way to acquire this knowledge is to study your own hands thoroughly. Look at the shape. What does it resemble? Pay particular attention to the thumb and how it relates to the rest of the hand.

If you have the ability, draw some hands in various positions. Even if your sketching ability is less than mine, you will learn a great deal from the experience.

There are several errors that are common to neophyte hand carvers. The most frequent error is carving the hands too small. The hands of most people are approximately as long as their faces. The width of a hand is about one-half its length.

Another error is the failure to make both hands the same size. This problem is easily solved with a little advance planning.

The third error is usually caused by a lack of knowledge. It's the failure to carve the planes of the hand in proper proportion.

The illustration represents the left hand in profile. Four planes, or flat areas, are shown. The first one extends from A to B and, in length, is one-half the total area from A to E. The second plane, B to C, extends from the first set of knuckles to the second set. The length of this plane is one-half the distance from B to E.

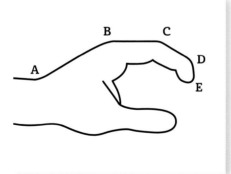

The third plane, C to D, is longer than the last plane but is not double its size. If you measure the last two planes of your hand you will find only a slight difference between the length of the two. However, when you carve a hand it's best to show a discernible difference between the two.

I had a discussion about hands recently with my friend Tom Bandoly. Tom is a Georgia compact character carver who uses the KISS method when he carves hands. His "Keep It Simple, Stupid" method is to carve a mitten and then separate the fingers. The system works for Tom because all his hand parts are proportionally correct and each part is in the proper position for what the hand is doing.

Each time you carve a hand, even if you use the "mitten" method, always draw the hand on the wood first. Cut away the waste wood that is around the roughed-out hand and make sure that ample wood is available to complete the hand.

Smooth the edges of the rough-cut hand and give it its final shape. Carve the planes on the backside, if that is appropriate, and separate the fingers. That's all there is to it.

The best way to learn to carve hands is to carve them on pieces of scrap wood. It's always better to goof up a practice stick than it is to butcher a carving. Don't be discouraged if your first tries aren't perfect; they don't have to be. Even if you have to throw away a few attempts, you will learn something valuable each time you try.

The hands that are in this section are some of the first "demo" hands I carved. They aren't great, but I often refer to them when I carve hands on my characters. It's easier to replicate a hand on a character if you have a "go-by" before you.

I would suggest that your first practice hand be a clenched fist (**Fig. 84**). From this pose, two other hands, which are pictured in **Figs. 85** and **86,** can be created with only a little alteration from the basic pose.

Carving a good fist will force you to carve the planes of the hand correctly. This, alone, is a major learning accomplishment.

When you have mastered all nuances of the fist, move the thumb from its clenched-fist position to a "thumbs up" attitude. The clenched fist, which is a symbol of strength, power, and/or anger becomes a sign that everything is "A-OK" when the thumb points upward.

Figure 84

Figure 85

Figure 86

Figure 87

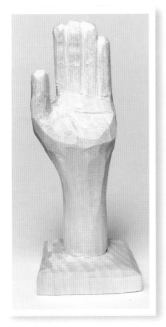

Figure 88

If you move the index finger outward from the fist, as in **Fig. 86,** several emotions can be expressed. When the finger is pointed at somebody or some object in the distance, it says, "Look at that!!!"

If it is pointed right at a person's face it means, "You #*#'!". When the arm and pointed finger are held aloft it expresses emotions such as, "We're Number One!!!", or "Hallelujah, Brother!!!" When other fingers are extended outward from the fist, they also express feelings or convey messages.

When the fist is relaxed a bit as in **Fig. 87**, an object can be inserted into the hole that was created. I usually rough carve the hand, drill a hole in it that is large enough for the prop, then complete the hand.

When the hand that is carved is holding an object, as opposed to having something inserted in a hole in the hand, the hand must be carved in a more open position. Examples of hands holding inserted objects carved with something in them can be found in the Rogues Gallery.

Fig. 88 portrays a hand with the palm in the up position. This hand, in my opinion, is much easier to carve than a fist. In figure carving, however, this side of the hand is seldom seen.

The backside of the hand, like the one in **Fig. 89**, is used often in figure carving. It's the hand that you see at the character's side or with thumbs hooked in his belt or flat against some part of his anatomy.

The hand displayed in **Fig. 90** is one of my favorite hands to carve. It is relaxed and cupped slightly. I carve it with the palm to the rear on an arm that is hanging down and slightly behind the character. Like most of the character carvers I know, my favorite way to carve hands is to put them in the character's pockets. Those hands are always perfect.

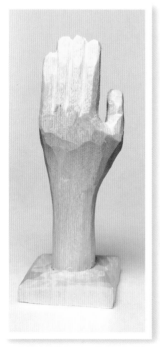

Figure 89

Figure 90

Maggie

CARVING 202
POST GRADUATE

DISPLAYING YOUR CARVINGS

Because the legs of your characters slant from front to back, the feet are large enough to give the carving a steady base. They will stand alone without tottering, but their smallness makes them easy to overlook.

Small characters are much more impressive when several are grouped together. When I was participating in shows in which I sold carvings, I exhibited them in antique type trays. I usually put twenty or more carvings in each of two trays, mounted the trays on art easels, and placed a display at each end of the table.

The system worked well for me. At each show I sold a goodly portion of my carvings. With an exhibit such as I described, people are prone to buy more than one carving at a time. I sold twenty or more of my little guys to a single customer on two different occasions. At each show several people found it necessary to buy two or more carvings because they couldn't decide on just one.

Another way to display your little guys is to mount them on small bases. Take the hunter at left, for instance. The base also gets him off the surface just a little bit.

When two individual carvings are attached to a flat base, an integrated carving is created. This draws even more attention to the piece because two characters are displayed together and the commonality of the two is established.

Occasionally, by carving a scene you can make something special out of a nondescript carving. For example, I carved a knight (Sir Gallant) that nobody wanted to buy. I carried him around for several years and couldn't sell him even at a discount.

I finally got tired of looking at that sorry specimen so I cut him up, scattered his parts on a flat base, smeared the base with lots of red paint (for blood) and black paint (for scorched earth), and gave it a caption that said, "Sometimes the Dragon Wins."

The scene, if you can call it that, attracts more attention than it deserves every time it is exhibited. This is a good example of turning nothing into something.

A CHALLENGE

At the 1996 Texas Woodcarvers Guild Spring Roundup I taught a two-day class for advanced carvers. The ones who enrolled in this class had attended my introductory class at least once. Some had taken it several times. All were experienced carvers.

I met with the group the evening before the day the class was to begin and gave each person two cutouts. I told them I was going to ask them to do something they had never been required to do before in any other workshop. The next morning they had to present an original idea for a two-person scene using the cutouts that were provided. All accepted the challenge.

The next morning each student had an idea and was prepared to carve a scene. At the end of two days, with only a little help from their instructor, most of the characters for the scenes were complete.

The patterns I used for the cutouts are shown below. The one on the left is a generic human. The one on the right is a generic something.

What was most interesting to me was the different characters that were carved from the patterns. The one on the left produced human males mostly, a few females, and even a bear with a camera. The pattern on the right generated everything from something human to nonhuman beings.

This turned out to be a fun experience for everyone in the class. The ideas that were presented were excellent and the carvings were appropriate for the scenes.

Only one person (a Rhode Island carver) produced an X-rated scene.

My challenge to you is to carve a two-person scene using each of the patterns at left and show it off to your carver friends. If you do so, you may as well make a certificate of completion for yourself that identifies you as a SMALL PERSON CARVER, FIRST CLASS.

How about it? Will you accept the challenge?

Harold, Medium Size Santa, and Radolf

RELIABLE SOURCES OF INFORMATION

A graduate student, as you may call yourself now, is expected to continue to pursue higher education by whatever means are available. You have, after completing this course, sufficient knowledge and experience to do this on your own.

A graduate student is also expected to belong to the National Wood Carvers Association and to his/her local and state organizations. Much is to be gained from membership in these fine groups and even more benefits are yours if you become an active, participating member.

As a part of your continuing education and pursuit of character carving excellence I'd like to recommend some books to you. These books are in my library and I use them as reference books.

Bolton, Claude. *Carving Heads, Hats and Hair.* Self published, 1986.

Cheek, Carl. *Drawing Hands.* Grosset & Dunlap. New York, NY. 1959.

Enlow. Harold. *Carving Western Figures.* 1984.

——. *How to Carve Faces in Driftwood.* 1978.

——. *Learn to Carve Faces and Expressions.* 1980.

Gauthier, Dick. *Drawing and Cartooning 1001 Faces,* Putnam Publishing Group. New York, NY. 1993.

——. *The Creative Cartoonist.* Putnam Publishing Company. New York, NY. 1989.

Hamm, Jack. *Cartooning the Head & Figure,* Grosset & Dunlap, New York, NY. 1974.

——. *Drawing the Head & Figure,* Grosset & Dunlap, New York, NY. 1976.

W. Pete LeClair. *Carving Caricature Heads and Faces,* Schiffer Publishing Ltd., Atglen. PA. 1995.

Maddocks, Peter. *How to be a Cartoonist,* Simon and Schuster. New York, NY. 1982.

Prescott, Steve. *Carving Blockheads.* Fox Chapel Publishing Co. Inc. Mount Joy, PA. 1996.

Redman, Lenn. *How to Draw Caricatures,* Contemporary Books Inc., Chicago, IL. 1984.

Wolf, Tom. *Carving a Friendship Cane with Tom Wolf and His Friends,* Schiffer Publishing Ltd., Atglen, PA. 1996.

——. *Carving Traditional Woodspirits,* Schiffer Publishing Ltd., Atglen. PA. 1996.

Vanderpoel, John H. *The Human Figure,* Dover Publications, Inc. New York, NY. 1935.

Thomas

ROGUES' GALLERY

Maggie

Hermes

Wise Riven

Gilbert

Brother Gasper

Dough

Thomas and Marvin

Radolf

Roy and Russell

Rogues' Gallery

Medium Size Santa

Ezequiel